Pacific Natural
At Home

JENNI KAYNE

Pacific Natural
At Home

Foreword by Vincent Van Duysen

RIZZOLI
NEW YORK

New York · Paris · London · Milan

CONTENTS

City

The Elements of Design

FOREWORD

by Vincent Van Duysen

For *Pacific Natural At Home*, Jenni has hand-picked a number of homes true to her interior design aesthetic and stylistic language. They are light-filled spaces serving as serene escapes for each of their owners; they boast minimal accents and thoughtful, yet pared back, characteristics. Nature takes center stage and invades the living quarters while feeding each of the tenants' inner tranquility.

I met Jenni in 2015, and it has been a story of two kindred spirits with common passions ever since. She was an admirer of the Flemish art of living, composed of desaturated colors, Belgian linens, and the purity of raw materials. I, on the other hand, have always been an admirer of mid-century architects, of the European modernists, and those who also operated in California.

The interiors in this book are symbiotic with
the design language that unites us.

INTRODUCTION

There's no place in the world I love more than home. From the bustle of Los Angeles to the quiet shores of Lake Tahoe, home is a place dedicated to togetherness, comfort, and family. It's a space for life's most special moments.

Every night, my family gathers around the dinner table. My kids, who range from toddler to preteen, join my husband and me as we each take turns talking about our days and sharing what we're grateful for. It's traditions like these, and all of the little moments in between, that make a house feel like a home.

I began writing this book during a time when home's importance was brought into focus for all, but my love for interiors is lifelong. I've always had a passion for the small details in life and the personal touches that make a space welcoming, beautiful, and special.

This book features the homes of amazing women I admire, each as unique and inspiring as the next. Every woman's home is a window into their world. By welcoming us into their spaces, we're offered a glimpse into how each woman articulates her own personal style and, more importantly, how she lives.

As much as *Pacific Natural At Home* is a showcase of inspired interiors, it's also a love letter to California. Broken up into four distinct landscapes of the state—canyon, ocean, valley, and city—each section aims to capture the essence of California living in its many forms. While the spaces throughout these pages are distinct in their own ways, each home finds common ground in the qualities I have come to love most about California style: its effortlessness, its embrace of nature, and its focus on comfort and informality.

There's a calming, freeing feeling evoked by the homes within this book. It's the California way. Cool, easygoing, and comfortable. I hope these pages inspire you to create that feeling for yourself, wherever you may be.

Canyon

Lost in the Landscape

Building a home is a true labor of love. The process is filled with inspiration, collaboration, and creativity. It takes time and patience, but the end result is worth the journey. Over the years, my family has grown, my husband, Richard, and I have moved farther west, and our taste has evolved. This home is a reflection of who we are, what we love, and all the memories that are to come.

From the plans to the build, we found the perfect match with Belgian architect Vincent Van Duysen, who worked in collaboration with Los Angeles firm Kovac Design Studio and landscape designer Christine London.

I have always admired Vincent's work from afar, and was very inspired by Belgian design and California architecture. To bring this vision to life, Vincent focused on plastered brick, plaster walls, oak, and soft, organic materials, centering the entire design around moments spent outside. The central courtyard provides constant light, and almost every room comes with a view. Built for our family, the layout flows and works perfectly in sync with the way we live. Windows in the great room open up to relaxed moments outside, where togetherness and well-being are central.

Our love for California living connects our entire home to its surroundings: weeknight dinners flow from the kitchen island to the vibrant yard, centerpieces are arranged in the garden, and kids are constantly running around outside. This space reflects all the moments that make life special.

Jenni's Tip: Break up the flow with asymmetrical pillow placement. Modern spaces feel more personal with imperfections that speak to you.

Jenni's Tip: My husband calls hardware the jewelry of the house. Try mixing finishes: we used bronze hardware and nickel faucets in the kitchen.

"My home is centered around beautiful moments. Windows open up to nature, and interiors are organic. The space was designed to feel relaxed, welcoming, and grounded."

—JENNI KAYNE

The California Countryside

When Emma Grede relocated from London to California with her husband, Jens, and two young children, the Good American CEO was focused on finding a welcoming space to create new family roots. The stars aligned, and they found a piece of the English countryside tucked away in the winding hills of Bel Air.

Originally built by Paul Williams, Emma's space took on new life with help from architect Scott Mitchell and interior designer Sandy Gallin. Emma and Jens consciously decided not to rush to furnish the house. Instead, they chose to take their time collecting meaningful pieces that would make their home feel like their own.

While every room comes with its own compelling point of view, the living room is the space that captivates. From the shearling-upholstered chairs to the marble tables, the medley of texture, tone, and shape is suited for a family of California creatives. Bright white walls sit in stunning contrast to the dark floors, wide windows effortlessly bring greenery in, and the doors are constantly open on the weekends.

Trading London for Los Angeles brought Emma's family a very welcome change: the weather. Their kids play in the pool while the ivy-wrapped pergola offers an easy retreat for onlooking adults, and the outdoor nook with William Haines sofas serves as Jens's open-air office. From the yard to the kitchen, every space in their Bel Air hideaway is designed for time together—it's the perfect slice of the English countryside under the California sun.

Jenni's Tip: A single color palette doesn't mean you have to lose intrigue. Layer materials like shearling, stone, and wood for depth.

"This beautiful house is made for enjoying life to the fullest with the people we care about the most: our friends and family. We're making memories here that will last a lifetime."

—EMMA GREDE

Jenni's Tip: If your space leans more traditional, don't be afraid to bring in modern pieces of furniture for unexpected edge and personality.

The Curator's Masterpiece

Inside every home is a story waiting to be told. For Sheila Bouttier's Los Angeles space, that story comes alive through artful narration and personal curation—a task certainly suited for the founder of L.A.-based design gallery Galerie Provenance. Using vintage artifacts and décor as her form of fiction, Sheila's space is a work of art made for bringing together those she loves most.

Sheila enlisted architect William Hefner for both the build and the landscape design to create a space that's modern in form and feel. The bones of the home set the stage for a gallery of wonders from one room to the next. Thirty-foot walls in the main hallway invite exploration as rich oak floors and intriguing accents guide guests with ease.

While everything feels polished, there is a sense of familiarity that connects you with the objects and design. From the vintage artifacts to the colorful details, each item in Sheila's home is eye-catching but never strays toward overbearing. This balancing act is something we can all aspire to re-create.

Pieces of the past ground her home's collective narrative, but the focal point of Sheila's space is the work of her late grandfather, artist Benjamin Abramowitz. From vibrant abstract paintings and nude drawings to personal sketches of her grandmother and mother, his artistic mark adds a layer of legacy and connection to the walls. Every room in Sheila's home works to tell the greatest story of all: her own.

Jenni's Tip: Put the same thought into your entry as you would your living room. Swap in new objects and display special pieces.

Jenni's Tip: Gallery walls are a great way to hang smaller pieces you love and express your personality. Lay your pieces on the floor to determine the right configuration and trust your intuition.

"From the 1960s Charlotte Perriand stools to the three-hundred-year-old Swedish root bowl—these pieces have a story. They have a past. They have soul. Whose hands have touched them? What have they witnessed?"

—SHEILA BOUTTIER

Ocean

The Bold Beach House

When Vanessa Alexander set out to design the Malibu home she shares with her husband, Steve, and their sons, she landed on a stylistic choice that made her beach house bold: she painted it black. For the interior designer behind Alexander Design, the decision was the final step in defining her take on the beach house aesthetic—but the layer of paint is just the beginning.

Vanessa is no stranger to Malibu and its celebration of outdoor living. Eager to capture the beauty of her surroundings, Vanessa made sure her space was relaxed and full of light. High ceilings with skylights let the light pour in from above, while walls of glass emphasize the landscape, blurring the lines between indoors and out.

The house was built from the ground up, and the finished product illuminates a fine-tuned process. Vanessa and Steve dreamed up their beachside vision with support from Kovac Design Studio and Terremoto, creating a home that reflects how their family likes to live: at ease, outdoors, and together. Regardless of the time of day, you're likely to find Vanessa and her loved ones in the kitchen and family room, where the open floor plan is perfect for seamless entertaining. From the hand-forged brass cabinetry to the striking pendant that hangs over the island, custom-designed pieces punctuate every room.

Finding a balance between luxurious and livable isn't always easy, but Vanessa does so beautifully. The skateboard ramp in the yard has as much importance as the Pierre Yovanovitch light fixtures and the turn-of-the-century farm table. Contrast is constantly at work, creating a space suited for the animated and active family with a penchant for exceptional design. Vanessa's enviable ability to make a highly designed space feel like home is what shapes her distinct version of coastal sensibility.

Jenni's Tip: If you're a frequent entertainer, keep an open flow from the kitchen to the family room with plenty of movable seating.

"I feel immediately inspired and at ease in the environment we have created. It's truly a haven and destination where my family and I can put away some of the stresses of the world."

—VANESSA ALEXANDER

Jenni's Tip: Keeping bedrooms quiet and clean by opting for organic and calming materials like oak, bouclé, and linen ensures that your space remains a restful retreat.

The Entertainer's Ocean Oasis

The kitchen is the heart of every home. That's certainly the case with Courteney Cox's Malibu retreat. Overlooking the ocean, her space is one of the most idyllic places to go to for a laid-back dinner party, celebratory evening, or casual weekend. Built by Kovac Design Studio to make the most of the view, almost every room opens up to the ocean as sliding glass doors work to epitomize the California feeling.

Courteney's home is marked by a seamless flow that allows guests to wander inside and out with ease. The spirit of the beach is amplified through organic features like wooden accents and stone-filled pathways, while landscape design by Coral Browning Gardens creates the ideal coastal environment. Every detail matters, but nothing is too precious as beach days turn into fireside evenings.

Working with designers Trip Haenisch, Cliff Fong, and, most recently, Clements Design, Courteney chose to forgo the beach house archetype of bright whites and blues, opting instead for darker, moodier moments. The informal yet elevated nature of her design choices ensures guests are always at ease, while rich tones and unique collectible pieces are mixed in faultlessly.

The family room connects the kitchen with the outdoors, giving friends and family the ability to lounge as Courteney cooks. In a nod to quintessential California living, the windows are always open, creativity is in constant motion, and entertaining is an everyday occasion. From poolside views to the alfresco dining room, this is a place you come to and never want to leave.

Jenni's Tip: Neutrals mean more than shades of beige. Find your core palette, using darker accents for a modern yet grounded feel.

"I feel extremely lucky to be able to open the door and see the vast view of the ocean. It makes me immediately stop and take a breath of gratitude."

—COURTENEY COX

Jenni's Tip: Think of open shelving as a gallery for your favorite ceramics to be enjoyed by all. If it's in your collection and on display, don't be afraid to use it daily.

A Minimalist Hideaway

The light in Julia Hunter's Venice home always seems to shine just right. With a simplified design that inspires a coastal state of mind, every inch of her space comes with its own distinct point of view. The sunny and pared-back interiors are no coincidence: as the CEO of Jenni Kayne, Julia speaks the language of California living every single day.

For Julia, her husband, Ray, and their young children, taking the time to adopt a less-is-more approach and aesthetic was a deliberate decision. With soft tones, custom oak floors, and strikingly subdued plaster walls, the stillness surrounding the space is impossible to ignore.

Designed by Hayden Slater, the space is representative of how we all aim to live. The kitchen, living room, and dining area work as one cohesive and open space, providing the perfect framework for inclusive and uncomplicated hosting, and the casual moments that make up each day. Minimalism may seem at odds with a busy family, but Julia's home finds a way to give every element its rightful place with effortless uniformity.

Nature's proximity informs the textures at work both indoors and out. White wooden beams in the pitched living room ceiling complement a well-kept stack of wood that sits in its alcove by the fireplace. Linen sofas and casual seating areas provide a cozy contrast to the decomposed granite and simple grasses outside. An olive tree in the corner links the indoors to the exterior. Whether you're inside or out, every element works to tell a cohesive story of the coast.

Jenni's Tip: It's easy to overdo the fireplace.
A simple plaster fireplace adds an organic,
modern feel to any home.

"I feel eternally grateful that my family has such a beautiful place to come home to. I want our loved ones to have that same sense of peace when they're inside our space."

—JULIA HUNTER

Jenni's Tip: A minimal bathroom can feel special with elevated hardware—a perfect reminder to pay attention to the details.

Valley

Desert Serenity in Adobe

Days are quiet in the California desert. For interior designer Sarah Solis, channeling this captivating quality is just what was needed to create this version of a desert oasis. Located in the open-sky setting of Pioneertown, the space provides a serene escape from the everyday by placing a focus on simplified and subdued living.

Designed by Sarah to match the landscape in its entirety, the space is a perfect example of all that a desert house can and should be. The overall feeling remains still and quiet, yet fully connected to the outside world.

The home's adobe bones date back to 1935. Rather than fill the space with modern updates, Sarah chose to mirror the pared-back priorities of the environment by focusing on clean, elemental materials. Adobe and concrete ground the space, while white oak cabinetry, plaster clay, and stone accents give each room a touch of lived-in ease.

A creative haven for musicians and artists alike, Pioneertown, with its Old West history and artistic energy, informs the design. Expansive living room windows face the mountains in a picturesque scene, built-in shelving and nooks keep practicality at the helm, and fireside details bring a touch of nostalgia.

But in classic California fashion, the true treasure exists outdoors: next to the swimming pool that seamlessly blends in with the desert scene is a sauna that faces the sun. No matter what the day brings your way, there are no worries to be had in this California escape.

Jenni's Tip: If you have an empty corner, bring native plants inside to connect the interiors with the landscape.

Jenni's Tip: Dress up the powder room with an antique floating sink finished with modern hardware.

"Now more than ever, we're looking for spaces to escape to and be surrounded by people we love and those who inspire us. This home is the best gathering place for that."

—SARAH SOLIS

The Matriarch's Forum

It's not uncommon for Suzanne Kayne's Palm Springs home to be filled with life. Grandchildren cartwheel through the halls, and the table is set for impromptu gatherings as everyone convenes in the open kitchen. While the scene might differ slightly from day to day, moments with loved ones are a throughline thanks to the space's welcoming design.

Family and friends always find their way to Suzanne's desert retreat—Molly Isaksen Interiors and landscape architect Joseph Marek made sure to take this mindset to heart. The house has an abundance of guest rooms and open living spaces, so being together is built in. Even during family-filled days, a sense of quiet remains with peaceful gardens and outdoor nooks.

Guest rooms take shape in the casitas around the main house, where reclaimed tile floors, washed linens, and Swedish antiques give each room a comfortable silence. Details like these define her space as a place that's thoughtful, functional, and at ease.

The family room, kitchen, and dining room all open up into one cohesive space, serving as the ideal layout for an ever-growing family. While every room is bound by a sense of community, the crown jewel of the home is defined by solitude and serenity: in the master bedroom sits a stone tub, nestled under an archway. The perfect retreat after a day of hosting, it's the culmination of a space made for Suzanne and her family.

Jenni's Tip: Sometimes a bare wall is more special than a busy one. Make your home its own centerpiece with design-forward walls and floors in materials like plaster and oak.

Jenni's Tip: It's important to choose a dining table that's suited for how you entertain: a round table for intimate family meals or rectangular for larger gatherings.

"I love looking around the house and seeing all the things we have collected over the years, whether it's a little painting we bought on a trip, or the silly bunnies my daughters make fun of me for. The house is filled with memories."

—SUZANNE KAYNE

A Designer's Daydream

An interior designer with unparalleled taste, Molly Isaksen built her desert home from the ground up with a flawless eye, choosing color and structure to honor both her natural surroundings and the modern architectural influence of Palm Springs. The finished product is an introspective experience designed for desert living.

Molly's design firm, Molly Isaksen Interiors, collaborated with Kovac Design Studio and Christine London to create an integrated design for the interiors, architecture, and landscape for her growing daughter and family.

By tapping into the desert sensibility, Molly's design choices feel both understated and meditative. With a color palette that mimics the landscape, the peaceful and empowering foundation makes you feel at home in an instant. Bright whites and clean lines may occupy the broader design, but the organic quality built into the space manages to maintain symmetry between composed and carefree. Even the pale travertine floors and custom furnishings are designed to be inviting with their light, bright feeling. While always practicing restraint, Molly creates a space made for living, which means nothing is too elevated to enjoy.

Situated around a central courtyard, her space is an ode to the outdoors. With careful consideration of the home's layout and surroundings, high ceilings and steel-framed windows and doors invite light in abundantly. As the sun shines throughout every corner of the property, it's hard not to relish the striking serenity of this desert getaway.

Jenni's Tip: A banquette in the kitchen can break up a more formal design. Don't forget about comfortable upholstery to add warmth.

Jenni's Tip: Exercise restraint. Sometimes all you need is a piece of pottery and some greens to make a space complete.

"One of the best things about living in Southern California is that you can really enjoy the outdoors all year long. It feels so luxurious, and so California, to sit inside by the fire with the doors open and the cool desert breeze blowing in."

—MOLLY ISAKSEN

City

An Homage to Hollywood

When conjuring up images of old Hollywood, Brigette Romanek's Laurel Canyon estate immediately comes to mind. Once home to music legends, the property she shares with her husband, filmmaker Mark Romanek, and their two daughters has rock 'n' roll in its bedrock. While balancing history and modern sensibility is no easy feat, Brigette took the challenge in stride and used her expertise to create a home in perfect harmony.

Rather than reinvent the space, Brigette worked with Ryder Design & Architecture to incorporate the home's quirks and history in a way that celebrates its inherent originality. Classic moldings bring character and personality as timeless tiles work to bring you back in time.

Inspired by the bones of the home, existing archways and marble floorings were not only kept intact—they were made the centerpiece of her modern adaptation. As the cornerstone of her artful approach, Brigette chose to focus on light. Early morning blue hues and the yellowish tones of the afternoon pour through the arched windows and doors of her curtainless living room. When the sun sets in Los Angeles, an afterglow fills every room, drowning the interiors in a soft California light.

Her impactful decorative decisions have an imaginative quality that crafts a unique narrative: natural patina works alongside sleek lines, and show-stopping works of art are instantly intriguing. By designing with an unbiased eye, Brigette finds a way to make sure each room is lived in equally. There are no favorites in this abode, just impeccable spaces to feel at home in.

Jenni's Tip: Plants aren't only made for corners.
Break up your space by placing a tree in the center.

"Living well is about dancing in the house to embarrass my kids, sitting at the dining table together, or on the edge of my girls' beds, and talking about life. Letting them know that in this home, there will always be love."

—BRIGETTE ROMANEK

Jenni's Tip: It can be instinctual to play it safe with larger pieces of furniture. Push the boundaries with statement-making materials and textures like burled wood.

Architectural Alchemy

Nancy Newberg had a vision: build a modular, hacienda-like home that combined different eras of design. With their kids grown and out of the house, Nancy and her husband, Bruce, were ready for something different. Working with architect Ron Radziner and interior designer Kathryn Ireland, Nancy created a light-filled Spanish-style home that's simultaneously modern and traditional, and always inviting.

Modernist Ron Radziner was enlisted to take two opposing sources of inspiration and turn them into a singular, actualized space. Spanish in style and modern in build, this space occupies a position that works beyond any sort of defined description.

Nancy's home is decidedly similar to the jewelry she designs: current yet timeless, neutral and detailed, all with a touch of texture. Softer moments of California design bring a comfortable and intimate minimalist feel. From her treasured pottery collection to the light fixtures that provide a modernist touch, each room thrives under artful design.

The space's relationship with the outdoors comes alive with landscape designer Stephen Block's work. Patios and decks are just as comfortably designed as the indoor spaces, adding a layer of seasonal spontaneity to every occasion. Rain or shine, Nancy and her family choose the outdoor living room over its indoor counterpart, a fact that feels fitting for a home that's effortlessly Californian.

"When my friends and family walk into my home, I want them to feel the same way that I do—like they have entered a peaceful and relaxing oasis."

—NANCY NEWBERG

Jenni's Tip: Think of an outdoor space as an extension of your indoors, and furnish accordingly: you'll be surprised by how quickly it becomes the center of your home.

Considered California Modern

Walking into Jessica de Ruiter's Silver Lake space is an experience that never gets old. Light moves about at an easy pace, setting the stage for minimalist moments. Built in 1953 by famed architect Gregory Ain, Jessica's home balances intent with a fresh perspective, resulting in a family home that celebrates the original vision.

Jessica and her husband, designer Jed Lind, were the ideal match for the historical home. Her stylist's eye paired with his design pedigree ensured that construction wouldn't lead to a complete renovation. Focused on maintaining the integrity of the original architecture, Jed designed the space with intention, highlighting the materials and moments that honored Ain's initial take: Douglas fir wood was restored, and exposed brick became a welcome backdrop.

Rather than rebuild to tack on square feet, they chose to restore their space in a natural way, tailoring specific elements to fit their family's needs. The wood-paneled wall in the office turns into a Murphy bed for guests, the kitchen island is minimal yet designed for family time, and their daughter James's bedroom flows into a multi-functional playroom with ease.

An imprint of modernism defines Jessica's home, which she embraces while bringing in her own preference for edited layers and depth. Whether you're gazing at the gallery wall or perusing the photos in the office, it's clear that every single object serves a purpose. From the upholstered built-ins to the personal collectibles that fill the space, each detail is aimed to ensure that Gregory Ain's original vision remains alive and well in the hills of Silver Lake.

"I love the natural light in California. The golden hour sunrises and sunsets are magical. Our home was built to let in tons of natural light, specifically the sunset over the hills at the end of each day."

—JESSICA DE RUITER

Jenni's Tip: Adding color to your space can be easy. Pick a shade to lead the way and find objects that work in synergy.

Jenni's Tip: Editing is a skill that takes practice. Pare down your space to just the essentials and let art and objects have space to breathe.

The Elements of Design

Design fundamentals and curated tips to bring the California-inspired
aesthetic to life in your own space.

The Anatomy of a Room

Every room in your home has a role, with each element serving a purpose that works in tune with your lifestyle.

The Living Room

Start with anchor pieces that are purposeful and reflect the way you live: the sofa, chairs, rug, and coffee table. Once I have the foundation, I layer in special elements and accessories.

I like choosing a piece or two that mixes it up and gives the layout a touch of the unexpected. Try floating a vintage chair on an angle, or positioning a table off-center.

If there's a rug you like but it's not the right size, try layering it over a larger solid natural rug so you can have the one you love.

The Kitchen

I like to display frequently used ceramics and wooden bowls on open shelves.
Mix it up by grouping bowls, mugs, and plates together, always with different
textures and glazes to create depth and interest.

I prefer natural stone countertops for subtle texture and a timeless look and feel.
A little wear and tear is normal, so embrace the imperfections.

It's common to focus on formal seating elsewhere, but everyday moments always
bring us to the kitchen. I love having stools at an island to keep it casual or a
built-in banquette for family meals.

The Dining Room

Focus on finding a table that works for your needs. If you entertain a lot, go for lots of chairs and a rectangular shape to accommodate everyone. If your life is centered around family dinners and intimacy, a round table is your best bet.

Height and width are important. You don't want guests sitting in chairs that don't fit comfortably or at tables that are too large for casual conversation. If you like to entertain family style, make sure the table is wide enough for everything to fit seamlessly.

Comfort is key. Source timeless and inviting seating that your guests will never want to leave.

The Bedroom

Focus on minimal furnishings with maximum functionality. Choose bedside
tables with enough storage to keep clutter out of sight, opt for lamps or
sconces that are practical for nightly reading, and never underestimate the
value of beautiful window treatments that filter in light the way you like.

Maintain the relaxed setting with bedding that doesn't need to be pressed
or perfect. Lightweight and versatile, linen is always an effortless choice.

Outfit your bedside table with thoughtful yet functional details like coasters,
trays, or catchalls to ensure your bedroom design stays intentional and tidy.
Add in a vase for flowers and a water carafe to complete your bedside story.

The Powder Room

I like to think of powder rooms as jewel boxes. For a room this small, the details make all the difference. One special element can completely change the space.

Find a vintage mirror or interesting light fixtures to give the room an elevated touch. I also love adding texture and warmth to a powder room with a small rug.

Focus on putting effort into the details: a vase with flowers, a silver tray with sentimental value, pottery, nice hand towels, and a beautiful bowl or coaster for soap.

The Neutral Color Wheel

A timeless palette grounded in neutrals gives way to endless possibilities for layering, tone, and texture.

PAINTS

Portola Paints
White Cliffs, Mont Blanc, Figueroa, Drop Out, Gem, Full Circle, Stone 1, Stone 2

Farrow & Ball
Strong White, Pointing, Dimity, James White, Wimborne White

Benjamin Moore
Barely There, Alaskan Husky, Steam, Gray Owl, Pure White

FABRICS, FLOORS & FINISHES

Fabrics
I love using natural, organic, and neutral fabrics. Linen, mohair, velvet, sheepskin, bouclé, leather, canvas, wool, and silk are constant favorites. Using an unexpected fabric in a neutral color is one of my favorite ways to keep things interesting and fresh while still using a quieter palette.

Materials
While specific choices vary by house and style, it's hard to go wrong with oak floors. I love stones like travertine, brick, terracotta, limestone, Calacatta, and Carrera. For a pristine and clean look, try corian or caesarstone.

The Art of Styling

From your coffee table to the open shelving in the den,
every surface in your space can tell a story.

THE COFFEE TABLE

Before you start styling, divide your surface
into four separate quadrants, spending time
on each one to ensure a balanced design.
Shift your items around to find a structure
that's organized and personalized.

Your coffee table can be a conversation starter.
Display books that sit with the palette of the
room and are meaningful and interesting.

Finish by layering pieces like ceramics, metal,
wood, or stone bowls and trays, followed by
special objects you want to see every day.

THE SHELVES

I try to create curated scenes with different vessels
and objects that vary in size, shape, and color,
such as books, bowls, and small pieces of art.

Play with the number of books you stack.
If your space is modern with cleaner lines, try
varying heights to break up any sameness.
If the rest of your décor leans more eclectic,
use the opportunity to create shapely structure.

Exercise restraint and give your items some
room to breathe. I find that there is always
beauty in asymmetry and purposeful space.

Curating & Collecting Art

No room is complete without the addition of art. Creating a visual language within your space is the best way to express your personal taste.

Explore galleries, auctions, websites, and books. When a piece speaks to you, find out the artist's name. Your love for a specific artist might be a great indicator of the period or genre you're interested in.

Take your time, purchasing pieces with the intention of creating a cohesive and long-lasting collection. If you truly love something, it's bound to work in any space you call home.

Invest in art that's going to hold its value. Trend-based pieces may lose luster over time, but works that are timeless or hold personal meaning will find value on and off the art market.

The Vintage Balancing Act

Mixing vintage with other pieces is the key to creating a space that's unique to you. There's a balancing act at work that delivers a look that's neither too polished nor too eclectic.

Let vintage fill in any gaps and serve as a balancing tool. If you have a new table, add in older chairs. Use vintage pieces to layer in moments where you need character, texture, or simply to mix it up. My dear friend who has impeccable taste calls this "turning the room on its head."

Look online, scour vintage stores, peruse flea markets, and reference books of eras or designers you love. The more you see, the more you'll understand what it is you like. Plus, vintage pieces don't always have to be costly.

Too much of anything detracts from the sense of novelty, so focus on timeless treasures that you'll love for years to come. Designer pieces will hold their value and should be treated like art. Let them stand out and feel special.

Bring Nature Indoors

Whether it's a visit to the farmers market or even foraging in your yard or neighborhood, adding elements of greenery livens up a space and brings the outdoors in.

HOUSEPLANT HOW-TO

These are some of my favorite, most reliable plants to bring indoors.

Full to mostly full sun:

Black Olive, Operculicarya Decaryi, Fockea Multiflora

Bright, indirect light:

Ficus Triangularis, Black Aralia, Ficus Lyrata, Ficus Audrey, Variegated String of Hearts, African or Baja Rock Figs

EVERGREEN ESSENTIALS

Bring branches inside when you need height, place a pot in the corner when something feels like it is missing, and scatter smaller vases throughout. I like to use mostly green foliage and mix in some blooms in the places that need an added detail or softening.

HOMEGROWN FAVORITES

Plants that I love include olive, almond, quince, and cherry branches, eucalyptus, rosemary, thistle flower, jasmine vines, white strawflowers, hydrangeas, bunny tail, bleached fennel flower, and geranium leaves. You can grow many of these outside and add them to arrangements with ease.

Celebrating Outdoor Living

California living is all about embracing the outdoors. Use the space you have wisely by thinking about your lifestyle and how you spend your time in nature.

Create a dining or seating area that will work for occasions big or small. Focus on shaded areas and furniture that will weather the seasons.

Utilize your space by creating special moments that you can discover or disappear to. Place benches in the garden and position chairs in areas that make the most of the view.

Make the most of the outdoors with pots and landscaping that are suited to your environment. Embrace the native plants and take note of other varieties in your neighborhood for inspiration.

ACKNOWLEDGMENTS

To Vincent

Thank you for the beautiful foreword and for designing our dream home.
You are an incredible talent and I am honored to call you a friend.

To my parents

Thank you for teaching me what a home should feel like and for surrounding
me with beauty, nature, and love from such a young age.
Everything I am today is because of you.

To my husband

Richard, thank you for our beautiful family and for being the most incredible
partner. Thank you for your Virgo eye and for appreciating all the small details
as much as I do. I am beyond grateful to you for finding our dream property,
exactly as I pictured and described it. I'm looking forward to many
memories and new traditions in our new home.

To Rip, Tan & Troop

Thank you for loving our traditions and helping to create new ones.
You make our house feel like home by filling it with energy and love.

To my friends

Thank you for your constant inspiration, support, and love.

To my sister Maggie

Thank you for sharing your eye with me, for introducing me to creative talent,
and for giving our home the gift of beautiful art.

To my sister Saree

Thank you for being my sounding board, editor, and inspiration in so many ways.

To my Jenni Kayne team

Julia, Sam, Meaghan, Jackie, Katherine, Cate, and John: Thank you for your tireless
work. You guys make it look effortless, always with a smile on your face. Thank you
for all that happens behind the scenes and for making this book come to life during
such a trying time. None of this would be possible without you.

To Angi

Thank you for taking the most beautiful photos and capturing all
of these women in their California spaces.

To Ellen Nidy, Charles Miers, and the team at Rizzoli

Thank you for your continued creative partnership and support.

To the beautiful women throughout this book

Thank you for letting us into your homes and your worlds. Thank you for sharing
your beauty and giving us all a glimpse into how you live.

CREDITS

PHOTOGRAPHY

Angi Welsch

Nicki Sebastian

Karyn Millet

Shade Degges

Kate Berry

PROP STYLING

Jackie Beyer

John Contreras

WRITING

Katherine Fox

ART DIRECTION

Cate Watchman

FLORAL DESIGN & STYLING

John Contreras

COPYRIGHT

First published in the United States of America in 2021 by
Rizzoli International Publications, Inc.
300 Park Avenue South, New York, NY 10010
www.rizzoliusa.com

Publisher: Charles Miers
Editor: Ellen Nidy
Design: Cate Watchman
Production Manager: Alyn Evans
Managing Editor: Lynn Scrabis

2022 2023 2024 / 10 9 8 7 6 5

Printed in China

ISBN: 978-0-8478-6964-0
Library of Congress Control Number: 2021938249

Visit us online:
Facebook.com/RizzoliNewYork
Instagram.com/rizzolibooks
Twitter.com/Rizzoli_Books
Pinterest.com/RizzoliBooks
Youtube.com/user/RizzoliNY
Issuu.com/Rizzoli